Planning a Funeral Service

A Guide to Planning a Funeral in the Episcopal Church

Jedediah D. Holdorph II

MOREHOUSE PUBLISHING

HARRISBURG, PENNSYLVANIA

Morehouse Publishing
P.O. Box 1321
Harrisburg, PA 17105

Morehouse Publishing is a division of The Morehouse Group.

The Scripture quotations contained herein are from the New Revised Standard Version Bible, copyright © 1989 by the Division of Christian Education of the National Council of the Churches of Christ in the U.S.A. Used by permission. All rights reserved.

All BCP references are to the Book of Common Prayer according to the use of The Episcopal Church.

Printed in the United States of America

Cover design by Rick Snizik

Library of Congress Cataloging-in-Publication Data

Holdorph, Jedediah D.
    Planning a funeral service: a guide to planning a funeral in the Episcopal Church / Jedediah D. Holdorph II.
        p. cm.
    Includes bibliographical references.
    ISBN 0-8192-1769-7 (paper)
    1. Funeral service—Episcopal church—Liturgy. 2. Episcopal church—Liturgy. 3. Funeral service—United States.
    I. Title.
    BX5947. B9H65   1998
    264' .030985—dc21   98–41906
                                                                  CIP

Contents

Introduction

If you are reading through this booklet, it is likely that you are doing so because someone you love has died, or because you are thinking ahead about the planning of your own funeral services. The material in this booklet should be helpful in both cases.

If you have recently lost a loved one, the Church shares your sorrow and stands ready to help. Planning a funeral is an overwhelming task, but it can also be a deep and immensely gratifying experience. What's more is that you need not do it alone. There are people to help—friends and family, of course, but also the funeral director and clergy. All of them want to work with you toward a befitting service for the one you love. I hope and pray that you will find a measure of consolation and comfort in the rites and sacraments available to you at this difficult time.

The basic form of a funeral service is provided for us in our Book of Common Prayer (BCP). The tone of the service itself is explained in a footnote to the service:

> *The liturgy for the dead is an Easter liturgy. It finds all its meaning in the resurrection. Because Jesus was raised from the dead, we, too, shall be raised.*
>
> *The liturgy, therefore, is characterized by joy, in the certainty that "neither death, nor life, nor angels, nor principalities, nor things present, nor things to come, nor*

powers, nor height, nor depth, nor anything else in all creation, will be able to separate us from the love of God in Christ Jesus our Lord."

This joy, however, does not make human grief unchristian. The very love we have for each other in Christ brings deep sorrow when we are parted by death. Jesus himself wept at the grave of his friend. So, while we rejoice that one we love has entered into the nearer presence of our Lord, we sorrow in sympathy with those who mourn.
(BCP 507)

As these words make clear, a funeral is a celebration—both of the specific life of the departed and of our common life in the risen Christ. And because the funeral is a celebration of our Christian hope, it is essentially an Easter celebration. The vestments worn by the clergy, therefore, are those worn at Easter. The colors on the pall that covers the casket in the church are those of Easter. The pall may also be decorated with symbols of Easter. The Paschal Candle, first lit at the Easter Vigil, is prominently displayed. Even the hymns sung are often chosen for their connection to the Easter season.

At the same time, funerals are times of intense grief and sorrow. As the Prayer Book points out, it would be profoundly unchristian not to care enough to grieve the loss of those we have loved and cherished. Many of the readings and prayers used in the service help make room for mourning the loss you feel.

Part One
Planning the Service

Any service requires preparation. Clergy, of course, make the final plans for church services, but they do this in consultation with family members, so that the service can be personal as well as a faithful expression of our Christian hope.

An Episcopal funeral is normally simple. For this reason, extravagant floral arrangements are generally discouraged at Episcopal funerals. This is also part of the reason behind the use of a funeral pall, since it obscures the simplicity or the grandeur of the casket. The plainness focuses our attention on our faith in God and asserts our common hope and equal status before the Lord.

Still, even the simplest of services entails a surprising number of decisions. This booklet is designed to help you make some of those decisions. If you are not an Episcopalian, some of the words used in the Prayer Book (e.g., "collect" or "homily") may be unfamiliar to you. The officiating minister (usually a priest) is available to clarify anything that is not clear, and to help guide you through this difficult but powerful planning process.

What follows is not intended to be comprehensive; instead, it is merely suggestive of some of the issues to consider in planning a funeral. Your priest will want to go through this booklet with you as you prepare for the specific service of which you will be a part.

Preliminary Questions

Location of the Service

Before you make specific decisions concerning the service, you must address general questions such as where to hold the service. There may be personal reasons why some people are inclined to hold a service at the local funeral home instead of at the church—lack of involvement in a local congregation, for example, or the expected presence of people from different faith backgrounds. These reasons will have to be given due consideration, of course, but apparent obstacles usually can be overcome through some sensitive planning with your priest.

For the most part, however, services at the church are encouraged. Our Prayer Book asserts: "Baptized Christians are properly buried from the church" (BCP 468, 490). It is worth noting that the rites and sacraments of the Church are not tied to a local priest or congregation; they are the property of the whole Church. We are not baptized into a local congregation so much as we are baptized into the Communion of Saints; so, too, we are not buried from a particular congregation so much as we are buried from the Church. Inasmuch as the mystery of a human life lies hidden with God, the Church's sacramental expression of God's care encompasses the mystery of the whole of our lives, from beginning to end, from baptism to burial.

Communion

As soon as we place the funeral within the context of the sacraments, the next question that emerges is whether the service should include communion. The liturgies of the Prayer Book assume the celebration of the Holy Eucharist, although there may be reasons for not having communion, including whether or not the service is held in the church. Even with communion, the service rarely lasts much more than an hour. Indeed, without communion, the brevity of the service (perhaps not more than thirty minutes) may cause the funeral to seem abrupt.

The celebration of the Eucharist within the context of a funeral can be a powerful source of comfort. For those who regularly partake of communion, it is a participation in the sacrament by which God sustains and feeds us throughout all our days. Even more to the point, for two thousand years the Eucharist has been the sacrament through which people of faith have experienced the risen Christ as present among them. Even for those who do not regularly partake of communion, it can be seen as a participation in that heavenly banquet that transcends time and space, one that includes those we love but no longer see. It is, therefore, a sacrament that celebrates our ongoing connections—with God and one another.

Rite I or Rite II

Another question concerns the language that will be used in the service. For those not familiar with the current Book of Common Prayer, a brief clarification may be helpful. For many of our liturgies, the Prayer Book provides a choice between Rite I and Rite II forms. The Rite I form (beginning on page 469) uses an older-style language that is in keeping with the 1928 Book of Common Prayer. To some, this language will feel more reverential than do modern words. The Rite II liturgy (beginning on page 491), on the other hand, is designed to be more contemporary. The language used will feel more accessible to those not familiar with the older Book of Common Prayer.

There are other differences between these two forms of the service. For example, the Rite I form prints the Psalms in the body of the service's text, making it somewhat easier to follow. The Rite II service allows more choices in the forms of the prayers used, making it somewhat easier to personalize.

Music

Music is not required for a funeral service, but its inclusion can be very powerful. Music adds a profound mood to worship, and it draws people into the liturgy in ways that words alone often fail to do. Personalizing the service by using some favorite hymns or music of the deceased can be particularly poignant.

There is a variety of moments during the service at which music or hymns can be used. Congregational hymns can be sung during the opening procession, between one or more of the readings, at the offertory, during the administration of communion, and at the closing procession. If hymns will be sung by the congregation, special care should be taken to choose hymns that will be supported by those in attendance.

Normally, all services celebrated at the church will utilize the parish organist (assuming that person is available). The church office and/or the officiating priest will probably make the necessary arrangements with an organist/accompanist. Other musicians—soloists, instrumentalists, and so forth—are sometimes used. If you would like additional musicians, discuss this possibility with the presiding priest.

The Entrance Rite

The service begins with an opening anthem, typically said or sung as the body is borne into the church. The Rite I service provides the text of this anthem (BCP 469). In the Rite II service there are two options for the anthem. The first is a more contemporary rendering of the same anthem used in Rite I (BCP 491). An alternative is the anthem on page 492; this second anthem is in the form of a responsive reading between the presider and the congregation. If the opening procession does not use one of these anthems, the service can begin with music, usually a congregational hymn.

Once everyone is gathered, a short prayer (or collect) brings the entrance rite to an end. The Rite II service offers three options for the burial of an adult (BCP 493) and two more for the burial of a child (BCP 494). The Rite I service does not provide the same range of options, but suggests only one option for the burial of an adult and another for the burial of a child (BCP 470).

Scripture Passages

Three readings are usually read. The Prayer Book suggests appropriate readings to be used, one from each—the Old Testament, the New Testament (i.e., an Epistle), and the Gospel. The text of suggested readings is provided later in this booklet, along with some brief comments on them. The BCP also suggests specific Psalms for use, following one or more of the readings. From time to time, other readings may be used in place of the suggested readings. These changes should be discussed with the presiding priest beforehand.

The Sermon

A sermon (or homily) is a response to the readings used in a given service. It is used to remind the congregation of the hope that any of us has at the time of death: "Because Jesus was raised from the dead, we, too, shall be raised" (BCP 507).

For this reason, eulogies are usually discouraged: to clarify the hope we have for those who have died, a hope not grounded in what any of us has done in our lives (or diminished by what any of has failed to do). Our hope is grounded instead in what God had done for us in Christ Jesus. Appropriate comments and connections between the life of the person and the readings, however, can often be worked into the service upon consultation with the priest.

One alternative is to structure personal comments into the time allotted for a visitation—sometimes referred to as a wake or a vigil—prior to the funeral itself. (Most commonly, the visitation is held at a funeral home, but there is no reason why the church could not be considered as an alternative site.) Together, with the use of "Prayers for a Vigil" (BCP 465-466), such personal comments provide a poignant way to conclude the visitation.

The Apostles' Creed and the Prayers

The service allows the option of saying the Apostles' Creed following the homily. This particular creed finds its origins in the ancient Church's baptismal practices. Its use at a funeral underscores the point that the God who claims us at baptism is the same God who holds us at the time of our death.

The Rite II service goes so far as to include the full text of this ancient affirmation of our faith within the text of the liturgy itself (BCP 496). Although not written out in the Rite I service, the text of the Apostles' Creed can often be added into the bulletin (or reference can be made to other places in the Prayer Book where the text is printed).

The Prayers of the People usually follow the creed. The forms for the prayers are provided in the respective rites (Rite I, pages 480–481; Rite II, page 497). Both forms allow for some measure of personalization by the inclusion of the person's name. The Rite II form also provides two possible collects that can be said at the end of the prayers (BCP 498).

The Eucharistic Prayer

If the Eucharist is to be used as part of the service, you will want to consider which Eucharistic prayer you wish to use. If you have opted to use the Rite I form of the burial office, you will probably want to continue with one of the two Rite I Eucharistic prayers. Of the two, Prayer I (BCP 333–336) is more in keeping with the version used in previous Prayer Books and is therefore probably the more familiar choice.

The Rite II liturgies provide four different Eucharistic prayers to choose from. Of these four prayers, Prayer A (BCP 361–364) is the shortest and easiest to follow for those not familiar with Episcopal services, since page changes are not required. The Proper Preface for Commemoration of the Dead is used in both Prayers A and B but not in Prayers C and D. Your priest can help you decide among them.

Concluding Rites

After communion (or after the prayers, if communion is omitted), the service continues with the Commendation or the Committal. The Commendation, as the title suggests, is the prayer in which we commend our loved one into God's hands. It is brief, but the process is much longer—arguably a lifelong process.

If the Committal takes place immediately, the Commendation may be omitted. The Committal is the graveside service, almost a separate (albeit very brief) liturgy of its own. In the Committal we commend to God the person we are burying (as in the Commendation) as we commit that person's remains to rest.

In addition to burial in cemeteries, provision is made for alternatives, including burial at sea or cremation. In fact, cremation is not only permitted, but it is becoming increasingly popular. It is also becoming more common for churches to establish a place (called a columbarium) to inter cremated remains within the confines of church property. This is often seen as a way to connect with an older tradition of churchyards that included a cemetery, thus emphasizing the Christian assertion that we are forever bound to God within the life of the Church.

Participation of Family and Friends

Family and close friends may find some degree of comfort by participating in the funeral service. The most obvious way in which we can recognize the close relationships of certain individuals and the deceased is to ask them to serve as pallbearers. There are, however, a number of liturgical roles that can be helpfully filled by other family members and friends. Although it is sometimes difficult to read at a service for someone you love, it can also be deeply gratifying. Even children can often be given a job to do that tells them that they are an important part of the grieving family.

At the very least, someone will need to read the scripture passages and prayers that have been selected. In addition, you may want to select those who will help administer communion. Others can serve as acolytes and ushers. The priest will help you determine what roles need to be filled and who might best be able to fill them. If you would prefer not to ask family or friends to assume these roles, the priest will undoubtedly be in a position to make the necessary arrangements.

Receptions

There is often a group or organization within the congregation who would like to help organize a reception for friends and family. The reception may be held at the church or at some other location. If you are interested, please explore the possibilities with the priest and/or church office.

Flowers

Beyond an altar arrangement, flowers are not generally used to "dress up" a funeral in the Episcopal Church. Family members will want to advise friends and other family members that additional flowers will not be necessary. It is usually possible to publicize the family's wishes to support a specified charitable organization in lieu of flowers. Such a recommendation may but need not include donations to the local church memorial fund.

If you are ordering your own altar flowers, check with the priest to see if there are any restrictions on suppliers or types of arrangements before finalizing these decisions. The church office can typically arrange to have a standard altar arrangement delivered to the church if the family would prefer not to make its own selection.

Fees and Suggested Donations

The rites and sacraments of the Church are part of its ministry. For this reason, they are not typically offered on a fee-for-service basis. The policies of congregations will, however, vary from place to place. An organist, on the other hand, may need to be hired for a funeral, and that expense may need to be borne by the family. Your priest should be prepared to advise you in these matters.

Even if there are no charges for the services of the church, you may feel that it would be appropriate to make some sort of donation to the church and/or its groups and organizations that are providing support for the service, reception, and so forth. Again, your priest should be able to help you determine what might be an appropriate expression of appreciation. If the cost of any of these services is a problem, please advise the priest; other arrangements can almost always be made. The sacraments and ministrations of the Church should not be restricted only to those who are able to pay for them.

Part Two
The Readings

The readings listed below are suggested for use at a funeral. On the following pages, the complete text of each passage is printed along with some background on each reading.

Old Testament

> Isaiah 25:6–9 (He will swallow up death forever)
>
> Isaiah 61:1–3 (To comfort those who mourn)
>
> Lamentations 3:22–26, 31–33 (The Lord is good to those who wait for him)
>
> Wisdom 3:1–5, 9 (The souls of the righteous are in the hands of God)
>
> Job 19:21–27a (I know that my Redeemer lives)

New Testament

> Romans 8:14–19, 34–35, 37–39 (The glory that shall be revealed)
>
> 1 Corinthians 15:20–26, 35–38, 42–44, 53–58 (The imperishable body)
>
> 2 Corinthians 4:16–5:9 (Things that are unseen are eternal)
>
> 1 John 3:1–2 (We shall be like him)
>
> Revelation 7:9–17 (God will wipe away every tear)
>
> Revelation 21:2–7 (Behold, I make all things new)

Gospel

John 5:24–27 (He who believes has everlasting life)

John 6:37–40 (All that the Father gives me will come to me)

John 10:11–16 (I am the good shepherd)

John 11:21–27 (I am the resurrection and the life)

John 14:1–6 (In my Father's house are many rooms)

Old Testament Reading
Isaiah 25:6–9

On this mountain the LORD of hosts will make for all peoples a feast of rich food, a feast of well-aged wines, of rich food filled with marrow, of well-aged wines strained clear. And he will destroy on this mountain the shroud that is cast over all peoples, the sheet that is spread over all nations; he will swallow up death forever. Then the Lord GOD will wipe away the tears from all faces, and the disgrace of his people he will take away from all the earth, for the LORD has spoken. It will be said on that day, Lo, this is our God; we have waited for him, so that he might save us. This is the LORD for whom we have waited; let us be glad and rejoice in his salvation.

Old Testament Reading
Isaiah 25:6–9

To this day, the act of sharing a meal is a sign of community. But what is true for us in our day was even more true of ancient cultures. In that context, if one offered hospitality, it was more than a matter of polite courtesy; the host was thereafter obliged to treat that person as family, honor-bound even to defend that person against his or her enemies. These commitments and obligations pertained even more when the simple meal was elevated to the status of a special banquet.

This reading from Isaiah envisions a time when God will be the host of a banquet that is given for all the peoples of the earth. Such a banquet, lavish as befits a feast given by "the Lord of hosts," would signal a communion between God and humanity, a communion that spreads among all peoples. Everything that separates us from one another and from God—death, tears, disgrace—would be abolished if true communion replaced separation and hostility.

The Christian Church understands the Eucharist partly in the light of this feast. In Christ, God still invites us to a meal in which we are joined to God. We sometimes refer to communion as a foretaste of a heavenly banquet, because it is a meal that joins us to all those in the vast Communion of Saints, across time and space. Whenever we gather to share communion, God removes the barriers and joins us to God, to one another, and even to those we love but see no longer.

Old Testament Reading
Isaiah 61:1-3

The spirit of the Lord GOD is upon me, because the LORD has anointed me; he has sent me to bring good news to the oppressed, to bind up the brokenhearted, to proclaim liberty to the captives, and release to the prisoners; to proclaim the year of the LORD's favor, and the day of vengeance of our GOD; to comfort all who mourn; to provide for those who mourn in Zion—to give them a garland instead of ashes, the oil of gladness instead of mourning, the mantle of praise instead of a faint spirit. They will be called oaks of righteousness, the planting of the LORD, to display his glory.

Old Testament Reading
Isaiah 61:1–3

These verses come from a section of Isaiah that is thought to have been written when the people had returned to the Promised Land after years of exile. Although they were glad to be home, life was not all that they had expected. Times were hard and life was difficult. These words, in particular, offer encouragement to a people who are discouraged.

This passage does not downplay the difficulties and pain of the moment, but it promises that another time is coming. It recognizes the appropriateness of attire intended for a time of mourning even as it promises a time ahead when other clothing will be more appropriate: "a garland instead of ashes, the oil of gladness instead of mourning, the mantle of praise."

Sometimes, when life is not going well, we are inclined to lapse into despair. We wrongly confuse the feelings of the moment with a fixed reality. These feelings can become oppressive, captivating, imprisoning. The "good news" of this reading is that now is not to be confused with forever. When someone we love dies, we naturally grieve. It is a good and appropriate response, but it is not the final response open to us. As the previous reading also suggests, grief can be relieved and even turned to joy in the end.

Old Testament Reading
Lamentations 3:22–26, 31–33

The steadfast love of the LORD never ceases, his mercies never come to an end; they are new every morning; great is your faithfulness. "The LORD is my portion," says my soul, "therefore I will hope in him." The LORD is good to those who wait for him, to the soul that seeks him. It is good that one should wait quietly for the salvation of the LORD. For the Lord will not reject forever. Although he causes grief, he will have compassion according to the abundance of his steadfast love; for he does not willingly afflict or grieve anyone.

Old Testament Reading
Lamentations 3:22–26, 31–33

This reading seems to hold a contradiction. It says that God is responsible for grief, yet it insists that the "steadfast love of the Lord never ceases." Perhaps it would be fairer to say that the author of this passage simply could not conceive of God's not being in charge of everything—good and bad—and yet was convinced of God's love, mercy, and salvation. If so, the passage can be seen as an acknowledgment of suffering and grief in the world, even as it asserts that God's final will for us is something else.

The passage also emphasizes waiting, an important part of the grief process. Planning a funeral is almost always done quickly. Even in cases where family members have to fly in from different parts of the country, one rarely has more than a couple of days to plan the service. The brevity of planning, however, does not mean that the grieving process will somehow be shortened. Grief takes time. Perhaps this passage, with its emphasis on the need to wait, serves as a reminder of the time we need to give over to our grieving. We should not make the mistake of thinking that we can put the death of a loved one behind us quickly. Even when a long illness prepares us, death still comes as a surprise. And the experience of grief will continue to surprise for some time to come.

Old Testament Reading

Wisdom 3:1–5, 9

The souls of the righteous are in the hand of God, and no torment will ever touch them. In the eyes of the foolish they seemed to have died, and their departure was thought to be a disaster, and their going from us to be their destruction; but they are at peace. For though in the sight of others they were punished, their hope is full of immortality. Having been disciplined a little, they will receive great good, because God tested them and found them worthy of himself...Those who trust in him will understand truth, and the faithful will abide with him in love, because grace and mercy are upon his holy ones, and he watches over his elect.

Old Testament Reading
Wisdom 3:1-5, 9

If you try to find this passage in your Bible at home, you may fail. It is from the Apocrypha, a collection of writings that is not universally accepted as part of the Bible. We use these readings in the Episcopal Church, however, because we find that God still speaks to us through them.

This passage is an excellent case in point. Although the writings of the Apocrypha are relatively obscure, this passage is chosen regularly for funerals. It speaks to us about both sides of the reality of human life and human dying—pain, suffering, and torment, as well as grace, mercy, and peace. When someone dies, especially someone close to us, the truth both confronts and comforts us. The truth, of course, is the inescapable reality of the death that hangs over all of us; yet the truth is also the irrepressible promise of our faith that strengthens us.

In today's world, it often seems that we pretend that we can beat death. The medical profession is often characterized (not always fairly) as working to sustain life at all costs, sometimes without regard to the quality of the life that is being sustained. There is, many feel, a fate worse than death. For some, and especially for those who suffer through years of chronic, debilitating illness, death can be a release. Then, truly, as the author of Wisdom observes, "their departure was thought to be a disaster, and their going from us to be their destruction; but they are at peace."

Old Testament Reading

Job 19:21–27a

Job said, "Have pity on me, have pity on me, O you my friends, for the hand of God has touched me! Why do you, like God, pursue me, never satisfied with my flesh? O that my words were written down! O that they were inscribed in a book! O that with an iron pen and with lead they were engraved on a rock forever! For I know that my Redeemer lives, and that at the last he will stand upon the earth; and after my skin has been thus destroyed, then in my flesh I shall see God, whom I shall see on my side, and my eyes shall behold, and not another."

Choices for the Funeral of:

Name: _____

Date of birth: _____

Date of death: _____

Next of kin: _____

Telephone number: _____

Presiding priest: _____

Number expected at service: _____

Service programs to be printed?   ___ Yes   ___ No

A. Service Options

1. ___ Church   or   ___ Funeral home

2. ___ Eucharist   or   ___ Burial Office only

3. ___ Rite I   or   ___ Rite II

Note: Rite I provides two alternative Eucharistic Prayers (I or II); Rite II has four alternatives (A, B, C, or D).

B. Music

Organist: _____

Prelude Choices: _____

_____

_____

_____

_____

Opening Procession: ___ Anthem (specify for Rite II only);

_____

or

___ Hymn (specify)

_____

Other Hymns: _____

_____

_____

_____

_____

Soloist(s) or Instrumentalist(s):

Other?

C. Readings

First Reading (from the Old Testament):

_____

Psalm or Hymn:

_____

Second Reading (from the New Testament):

_____

Psalm or Hymn:

_____

Gospel:

_____

D. Other Service Details

1. Apostles' Creed   ___ Yes   ___ No

2. Collects (Rite II only)

   Opening Collect (p. 493 or 494) _____

   Collect at the Prayers (p. 498) _____

3. Lord's Prayer (Rite II only)

   ___ Traditional   or   ___ Contemporary

E. Participants

    Lector for the First Reading: _____

    Lector for the Second Reading: _____

    Reader of the Prayers: _____

    Chalice Bearer(s)   _____

    Acolyte(s)   _____

F. Flower Arrangements

    ___ by family   or   ___ by church office

G. Reception desired?   ___ Yes   ___ No

If yes, where would the reception be held?

Old Testament Reading
Job 19:21–27a

In the Book of Job we wrestle with the question of human suffering. In the opening chapters, Job, an undeniably good man, loses everything—his wealth, his family, and his health. The rest of the story details how he and others respond to such calamity. Job's friends offer their opinions, telling him that he must have done something wrong to merit such punishment. They advise him to amend his ways and turn to God for forgiveness. Furthermore, they assert that because God is good Job should not be angry. He should "get over it."

The portion of the story suggested for our use is part of Job's response to his friends. One presumes that Job's friends are well-intentioned, but their words do not offer comfort, and so he rejects their pious-sounding advice. In our own day, friends might say things that are less than helpful, and at times, downright hurtful. Their comments, like those of Job's friends, fail to comfort.

It might be helpful to remember the faith of Job in such times, a faith that allowed him to reject the bad advice of others and that pushed him to vent his anger. At the end of the Book of Job, God vindicates Job's faith. God's answer still leaves Job (and us) with the mystery of suffering and evil in the world, but God comes to Job and responds. We, too, are given permission to be angry with God and still be faithful. God will not abandon us because we are honest about how we feel. In fact, perhaps it is only by being honest with God that we can expect God to be present to us.

New Testament Reading
Romans 8:14–19, 34–35, 37–39

All who are led by the Spirit of God are children of God. For you did not receive a spirit of slavery to fall back into fear, but you have received a spirit of adoption. When we cry, "Abba! Father!" it is that very Spirit bearing witness with our spirit that we are children of God, and if children, then heirs, heirs of God and joint heirs with Christ—if, in fact, we suffer with him so that we may also be glorified with him. I consider that the sufferings of this present time are not worth comparing with the glory about to be revealed to us. For the creation waits with eager longing for the revealing of the children of God; Who is to condemn? It is Christ Jesus, who died, yes, who was raised, who is at the right hand of God, who indeed intercedes for us. Who will separate us from the love of Christ? Will hardship, or distress, or persecution, or famine, or nakedness, or peril, or sword? No, in all these things we are more than conquerors through him who loved us. For I am convinced that neither death, nor life, nor angels, nor rulers, nor things present, nor things to come, nor powers, nor height, nor depth, nor anything else in all creation, will be able to separate us from the love of God in Christ Jesus our Lord.

New Testament Reading
Romans 8:14–19, 34–35, 37–39

The readings from the Old Testament speak to us of themes that are common to the Judeo-Christian tradition. In this and the following readings, however, we can see some distinctively Christian themes introduced. This particular passage presents three central themes that are evident in many of the readings that follow. First, the incarnation of Christ attests to a God who has compassion on our suffering. This is not a detached and remote God. Secondly, the importance of baptism is highlighted as the means by which we are claimed by God forever. And thirdly, as a result of our Christian identity, we draw encouragement from the pattern of Christ's death and resurrection. More will be said about each of these (and other) themes in the pages that follow. It is enough to note that they are fully present here as well.

But what is most distinctive about this passage, of course, is the unmatched eloquence of Paul's words to describe the power of Christian faith. The reading acknowledges that suffering is an inevitable part of life. It goes on, however, to contrast suffering with the hope of that which is yet to be revealed to us. To be fully appreciated, these words must be spoken aloud—slowly, dramatically, deliberately.

New Testament Reading
1 Corinthians 15:20–26, 35–38, 42–44, 53–58

Christ has been raised from the dead, the first fruits of those who have died. For since death came through a human being, the resurrection of the dead has also come through a human being; for as all die in Adam, so all will be made alive in Christ. But each in his own order: Christ the first fruits, then at his coming those who belong to Christ. Then comes the end, when he hands over the kingdom to God the Father, after he has destroyed every ruler and every authority and power. For he must reign until he has put all his enemies under his feet. The last enemy to be destroyed is death. But someone will ask, "How are the dead raised? With what kind of body do they come?" Fool! What you sow does not come to life unless it dies. And as for what you sow, you do not sow the body that is to be, but a bare seed, perhaps of wheat or of some other grain. But God gives it a body as he has chosen, and to each kind of seed its own body. So it is with the resurrection of the dead. What is sown is perishable, what is raised is imperishable. It is sown in dishonor, it is raised in glory. It is sown in weakness, it is raised in power. It is sown a physical body, it is raised a spiritual body. If there is a physical body, there is also a spiritual body. For this perishable body must put on imperishability, and this mortal body must put on immortality. When this perishable body puts on imperishability, and this mortal body puts on immortality, then the saying that is written will be fulfilled: "Death has been swallowed up in victory." "Where, O death, is your victory? Where, O death, is your sting?" The sting of death is sin, and the power of sin is the law. But thanks be to God, who gives us the victory through our Lord Jesus Christ. Therefore, my beloved, be steadfast, immovable, always excelling in the work of the Lord, because you know that in the Lord your labor is not in vain.

New Testament Reading

1 Corinthians 15:20–26, 35–38, 42–44, 53–58

This passage opens with the explicit affirmation that the Christian hope is grounded in Christ's death and resurrection. Hence, the Prayer Book's understanding of the nature of a Christian funeral:

> The liturgy for the dead is an Easter liturgy. It finds all its meaning in the resurrection. Because Jesus was raised from the dead, we, too, shall be raised. (BCP 507)

The gospel accounts of Easter morning are amazingly varied. In some cases, such as when Jesus demands food and drink (Luke 24:41–43), a given passage emphasizes the physicality of Jesus' resurrected body. In other cases, he passes through locked doors (John 20:19,26). At times, Jesus is immediately and unmistakably recognized as himself (Matthew 28:9,17); at other times, he is recognized only after long conversation or as he chooses to reveal himself (Luke 24:13–31; John 20:11–16; 21:4–7). What is clear, however, is that Jesus himself is still the same person (marked by the marks of his crucifixion and identified by the relationships he established before his death), even if his body is somehow different.

What St. Paul proclaims in this passage, and what the Church reaffirms, is a belief in the resurrection of the dead. Paul details many ways in which our resurrected bodies will be different from what we now know—just as a fully developed plant differs from its seed. But even so, the plant necessarily bears some relationship to the seed from which it grew. So it will be with us also. For that reason, we show respect and reverence for the remains of those we bury or cremate, even as we look forward to the resurrection of the dead.

New Testament Reading

2 Corinthians 4:16–5:9

We do not lose heart. Even though our outer nature is wasting away, our inner nature is being renewed day by day. For this slight momentary affliction is preparing us for an eternal weight of glory beyond all measure, because we look not at what can be seen but at what cannot be seen; for what can be seen is temporary, but what cannot be seen is eternal. For we know that if the earthly tent we live in is destroyed, we have a building from God, a house not made with hands, eternal in the heavens. For in this tent we groan, longing to be clothed with our heavenly dwelling—if indeed, when we have taken it off we will not be found naked. For while we are still in this tent, we groan under our burden, because we wish not to be unclothed but to be further clothed, so that what is mortal may be swallowed up by life. He who has prepared us for this very thing is God, who has given us the Spirit as a guarantee. So we are always confident; even though we know that while we are at home in the body we are away from the Lord—for we walk by faith, not by sight. Yes, we do have confidence, and we would rather be away from the body and at home with the Lord. So whether we are at home or away, we make it our aim to please him.

New Testament Reading
2 Corinthians 4:16–5:9

We go through most of life as if nothing could stop us. We take aspirin to allow us to work through our headaches and sniffles. We insulate ourselves in climate-controlled cars, homes, and offices in order to carry on through lousy weather. Because we control so many elements of our environment, an encounter with death can violate our normal ways of doing things. Faced with the reality of death, we are faced with our ultimate lack of control. Using the imagery of this passage, mortality strips away our illusions.

But at the same time, death can also lay bare a longing deep at our center, one that is often hidden beneath all of the illusions that get us through our daily lives. Again, returning to the imagery used by Paul in this passage, we may discover ourselves "longing to be clothed with our heavenly dwelling." As painful as the stripping away may be, it may also reveal something we usually ignore. We discover that we are vulnerable and desirous of someone or something that can provide true security: "We wish not to be unclothed but to be further clothed, so that what is mortal may be swallowed up by life." The longing is real, not just wishful thinking. Just as we have been given tear glands that allow us to cry, we have hearts that allow us to long "to be further clothed." We long for a security that only God can provide.

This reading may seem especially apt after a prolonged and severe illness. Anyone who witnesses one whose "outer nature is wasting away," as Paul puts it, is pained. Those who love and care for someone seriously ill "groan" with them as their "earthly tent . . . is destroyed," longing for their pain and suffering to be "swallowed up by life."

New Testament Reading
1 John 3:1–2

See what love the Father has given us, that we should be called children of God; and that is what we are. The reason the world does not know us is that it did not know him. Beloved, we are God's children now; what we will be has not yet been revealed. What we do know is this: when he is revealed, we will be like him, for we will see him as he is.

New Testament Reading
1 John 3:1–2

It may come as a surprise that the readings suggested for a funeral don't say more about what to expect after death. Rather, they are somewhat circumspect about their descriptions of the resurrected life. The Christian faith, it would seem, does not require a narrow, specific belief in the nature of heaven and hell, but allows for a certain modest uncertainty, since "what we will be has not yet been revealed."

But despite this reluctance to speak in overly specific detail about what to expect, these readings are full of confidence. As this passage says, that confidence is borne not of the knowledge of a specific future, but rather of the love revealed to us already. These readings may leave the mystery of what happens to us beyond the grave, but they all point to a God who loves us as a parent loves a child.

When Jesus was baptized, a voice announced to him, "You are my Son, the Beloved; with you I am well pleased" (Luke 3:22). As this passage bears out, the voice of God rings those same words to us at baptism, saying to those being baptized, "You are my son, my daughter, my beloved; with you I am well pleased." Just as that affirmation at the beginning of Jesus' earthly ministry was the ground of his ministry, so, too, is it for us. "Beloved, we are God's children now" is the affirmation we all receive from God at our beginning; it is the affirmation that carries us through to our ending. The love of God is both our starting point and our resting point, both our hope and our calling.

New Testament Reading
Revelation 7:9–17

After this I looked, and there was a great multitude that no one could count, from every nation, from all tribes and peoples and languages, standing before the throne and before the Lamb, robed in white, with palm branches in their hands. They cried out in a loud voice, saying, "Salvation belongs to our God who is seated on the throne, and to the Lamb!" And all the angels stood around the throne and around the elders and the four living creatures, and they fell on their faces before the throne and worshiped God, singing, "Amen! Blessing and glory and wisdom and thanksgiving and honor and power and might be to our God forever and ever! Amen." Then one of the elders addressed me, saying, "Who are these, robed in white, and where have they come from?" I said to him, "Sir, you are the one that knows." Then he said to me, "These are they who have come out of the great ordeal; they have washed their robes and made them white in the blood of the Lamb. For this reason they are before the throne of God, and worship him day and night within his temple, and the one who is seated on the throne will shelter them. They will hunger no more, and thirst no more; the sun will not strike them, nor any scorching heat; for the Lamb at the center of the throne will be their shepherd, and he will guide them to springs of the water of life, and God will wipe away every tear from their eyes."

New Testament Reading
Revelation 7:9–17

The Book of Revelation is a difficult book for many people to-day. It is written in a distinctive and unusual literary form known as apocalyptic literature. This genre, filled with symbolic imagery, was very common in biblical times but is less familiar in our own time. Because of its unusual imagery, Revelation can seem to be downright disturbing at times.

Some interpreters of the Bible see the Book of Revelation as a predictor of the world's end. Others have concluded that such an understanding misses the point. Read within the biblical context, Revelation was written for a people being persecuted for their beliefs; its use of cryptic symbols helped to obscure its meaning from hostile authorities. But for believers who understood the symbols, Revelation offered hope in the midst of travail. Understood this way, it may also offer a word of hope to us in the midst of our own travails.

Written at a time when the future of believers seemed anything but secure, the passage speaks of a hope beyond those present circumstances. It envisions this final hope not as something reserved for just a select few, but for "a great multitude that no one could count, from every nation, from all tribes and peoples and languages." The early Christians were encouraged to look for consolation beyond their difficult and fearful circumstances. We, too, can take comfort from this vision, knowing that there will come a time when all afflictions are rendered inconsequential by God, who reaches out to us and wipes away every tear.

New Testament Reading
Revelation 21:2-7

And I saw the holy city, the new Jerusalem, coming down out of heaven from God, prepared as a bride adorned for her husband. And I heard a loud voice from the throne saying, "See, the home of God is among mortals. He will dwell with them as their God; they will be his peoples, and God himself will be with them; he will wipe every tear from their eyes. Death will be no more; mourning and crying and pain will be no more, for the first things have passed away." And the one who was seated on the throne said, "See, I am making all things new." Also he said, "Write this, for these words are trustworthy and true." Then he said to me, "It is done! I am the Alpha and the Omega, the beginning and the end. To the thirsty I will give water as a gift from the spring of the water of life. Those who conquer will inherit these things, and I will be their God and they will be my children."

New Testament Reading
Revelation 21:2–7

In the opening verses of the Book of Revelation, John reports that what follows is part of an ecstatic vision. It might be helpful to consider it like a dream (an altered state of consciousness with which we are more familiar). In visions and dreams we don't expect the meaning to necessarily be self-evident or literal, but that doesn't mean a dream is not profoundly true. There is a difference between fact and truth. Consider the truth of Martin Luther King Jr.'s announcement, "I have been to the mountaintop!" His "dream" was profoundly true, even if it was neither a literal statement nor a reality that he would see come into existence in his time (or even in our own).

That's the kind of truth we find in this passage. It describes a time when the separations we experience will be overcome by communion. God will dwell with us and will remove all our afflictions. The hope spelled out here is true, even if it is not a literal description of what we are experiencing right now. In the midst of our grief, it may seem impossible to believe that "mourning and crying and pain will be no more," and yet the dream calls us to strive toward that place that seems so far away.

Another truth held out to us in this passage is hidden in its description of God as "Alpha and Omega." Of course, this doesn't mean that God is literally the first and last letters of the Greek alphabet. Instead, it means that God is present throughout all of life—in all places and at all times, from beginning to end. This passage encourages us to see that God is present in the whole of life—in our living and in our dying.

Gospel Reading
John 5:24–27

Jesus said, "Very truly, I tell you, anyone who hears my word and believes him who sent me has eternal life, and does not come under judgment, but has passed from death to life. Very truly, I tell you, the hour is coming, and is now here, when the dead will hear the voice of the Son of God, and those who hear will live. For just as the Father has life in himself, so he has granted the Son also to have life in himself; and he has given him authority to execute judgment, because he is the Son of Man."

Gospel Reading

John 5:24–27

In this passage, eternal life is not merely something to look forward to after we die; it is a reality open to us while we are still breathing. As Christians, we affirm that Jesus gives us our entry into that life. In one of the Eucharistic prayers we give thanks to God, saying, "you, in your mercy, sent Jesus Christ, your only and eternal Son, to share our human nature, to live and die as one of us, to reconcile us to you, the God and Father of all (BCP 362)." This takes place in the here and now before it ever becomes an issue in the hereafter.

Eternal life is fundamentally a life lived in communion with God, the source of all life. Jesus' capacity to live this kind of life is what freed him from being captivated by a fear of death and the judgment of others. Having "life in himself," Jesus did not derive his life from others, and he did not need to conform to the standards and expectations of others. This freed him to embrace all of life and everyone who lives. In crucifying Jesus, the world tried to render judgment against him. Their judgment seemed to be the end of the matter, but the resurrection announced God's vindication of all that for which Jesus lived and died.

Because Jesus comes to us as the one who reconciles us to God and gives us life, we, too, are encouraged to face both life and death without fear of judgment. After all, the judge is none other than Jesus, who is the source of our life. That is why we have confidence at the time of death. Judgment, in the final analysis, belongs to none other than Christ, who has already promised us the gift of eternal life, starting now.

Gospel Reading
John 6:37–40

Jesus said, "Everything that the Father gives me will come to me, and anyone who comes to me I will never drive away; for I have come down from heaven, not to do my own will, but the will of him who sent me. And this is the will of him who sent me, that I should lose nothing of all that he has given me, but raise it up on the last day. This is indeed the will of my Father, that all who see the Son and believe in him may have eternal life; and I will raise them up on the last day."

Gospel Reading

John 6:37–40

This passage describes the hope and promise that is ours as part of the Christian family that we are adopted into at baptism. Picking up on imagery found throughout the New Testament, baptism is sometimes described as an adoption into God's family. We are free to leave that family as we "grow up," just as we are free to leave our biological families—to move away from home, to change our names if we want to. But, for all of that, we cannot really change our identity. We are still the son or daughter of our mother and father. So, too, once we have been adopted into God's family, we will always remain God's children. We may stop coming home on weekends to gather around God's table with other members of the family, or we may stop going by the family name of "Christian," but God still claims us and will never, as Jesus puts it, drive us away. As the Prayer Book says in its description of the rite of Holy Baptism: "The bond which God establishes in Baptism is indissoluble" (BCP 298).

In the preface to the funeral service, the Prayer Book suggests this Gospel passage as the most appropriate for the burial of an infant or child. In baptism and in burial, we fall back on the same hope. In both cases, we trust God, who claims us as children with Christ—claimed first at baptism and then in a final way at burial.

Gospel Reading
John 10:11–16

Jesus said, "I am the good shepherd. The good shepherd lays down his life for the sheep. The hired hand, who is not the shepherd and does not own the sheep, sees the wolf coming and leaves the sheep and runs away—and the wolf snatches them and scatters them. The hired hand runs away because a hired hand does not care for the sheep. I am the good shepherd. I know my own and my own know me, just as the Father knows me and I know the Father. And I lay down my life for the sheep. I have other sheep that do not belong to this fold. I must bring them also, and they will listen to my voice. So there will be one flock, one shepherd."

Gospel Reading
John 10:11–16

The good shepherd image of Jesus comes from the biblical understanding of "Shepherd-God": the relationship between God and God's people is likened to the one between a shepherd and his/her sheep.

Jesus knew of this rich tradition when he described himself as the good shepherd. He also knew (as we perhaps do not) of its full significance. Because of the distance that lies between us and Palestinian shepherds of biblical times, we fail to hear and understand the full meaning of the tradition. Palestinian shepherds didn't graze their sheep on green hillsides. Rather, they tended their sheep in a rocky desert, having to search for sparse tufts of grass and all the time watch for predators and other dangers. What's more, these shepherds didn't fatten sheep for slaughter, but instead raised them for their wool. The sheep were not commodities for a season; they were companions for life. They were not just a shepherd's livelihood; they were his life. Of course he would give himself for them, for without them he would be nothing. That is the full measure of Jesus' commitment and connection to us. It is a commitment that he makes not only to those who are obvious members in good standing, but also to all he considers part of his flock, including those "that do not belong to this fold."

Gospel Reading
John 11:21–27

Martha said to Jesus, "Lord, if you had been here, my brother would not have died. But even now I know that God will give you whatever you ask of him." Jesus said to her, "Your brother will rise again." Martha said to him, "I know that he will rise again in the resurrection on the last day." Jesus said to her, "I am the resurrection and the life. Those who believe in me, even though they die, will live, and everyone who lives and believes in me will never die. Do you believe this?" She said to him, "Yes, Lord, I believe that you are the Messiah, the Son of God, the one coming into the world."

Gospel Reading
John 11:21–27

This passage is a brief excerpt of a longer narrative. Martha and her sister, Mary, had already sent word to Jesus that Lazarus was ill, but Jesus delayed his return. When he finally arrives, Lazarus has been dead for four days. And so Martha greets him with a rebuke, "Lord, if you had been here, my brother would not have died." When Mary greets him (verse 32), she is even more abrupt.

When we watch someone we love take ill and die, it may seem that God's response is slow in coming. It may help us to hear that faith does not preclude our being angry or confused about why this is so. Faith does not mean hiding our real feelings from God. On the contrary, faith makes room for us to give voice to those feelings and share them. There is room for our sorrow and pain as well. When Jesus finally goes to the tomb, he weeps. This tells us that our suffering is not ours alone; God shares it with us. We need not hide our feelings as if they were inappropriate.

In the end, when Jesus raises Lazarus, he enlists the help of others. Presumably, the power that could calm the seas and raise the dead could have done this by himself, but he doesn't. Jesus asks others to move the stone beforehand. He asks others to take off the burial wrappings afterward: "Unbind him, and let him go" (verse 44). So, too, we need not go through this process alone. There are others to help along the way.

Gospel Reading
John 14:1–6

Jesus said, "Do not let your hearts be troubled. Believe in God, believe also in me. In my Father's house there are many dwelling places. If it were not so, would I have told you that I go to prepare a place for you? And if I go and prepare a place for you, I will come again and will take you to myself, so that where I am, there you may be also. And you know the way to the place where I am going." Thomas said to him, "Lord, we do not know where you are going. How can we know the way?" Jesus said to him, "I am the way, and the truth, and the life. No one comes to the Father except through me."

Gospel Reading
John 14:1–6

This passage records part of what was said between Jesus and his disciples on the night before Jesus' betrayal and crucifixion. On the eve of his own death, Jesus offers words that provide his disciples a measure of comfort in the difficult times that lay ahead. He tells them of his imminent death and promises that it will not lead to separation but rather to a deepened fellowship—with himself and ultimately with one another.

Some of the disciples received Jesus' words with silence and others with promises to remain by Jesus' side, whatever might happen. But Thomas had a different response: He voiced his confusion and uncertainty. Because of Thomas' response to Jesus here, and even more so because of his response upon hearing of Jesus' resurrection three days later, he is commonly known as "doubting Thomas." This, however, is not an entirely fair description. Indeed, it is worth remembering that although Peter put on a brave front and promised not to deny Jesus, he failed miserably. Given Peter's failure, perhaps Thomas's model is a better one for us to heed. When all is said and done, Jesus does not chastise Thomas for his confusion; instead, he simply responds to Thomas by offering himself as the answer.

The Christian attitude of hope is, in the end, neither one of pretense nor despair. Rather, our hope is in touch with the reality and pain of death, even as it is full, because it knows that sorrow is not the final word.